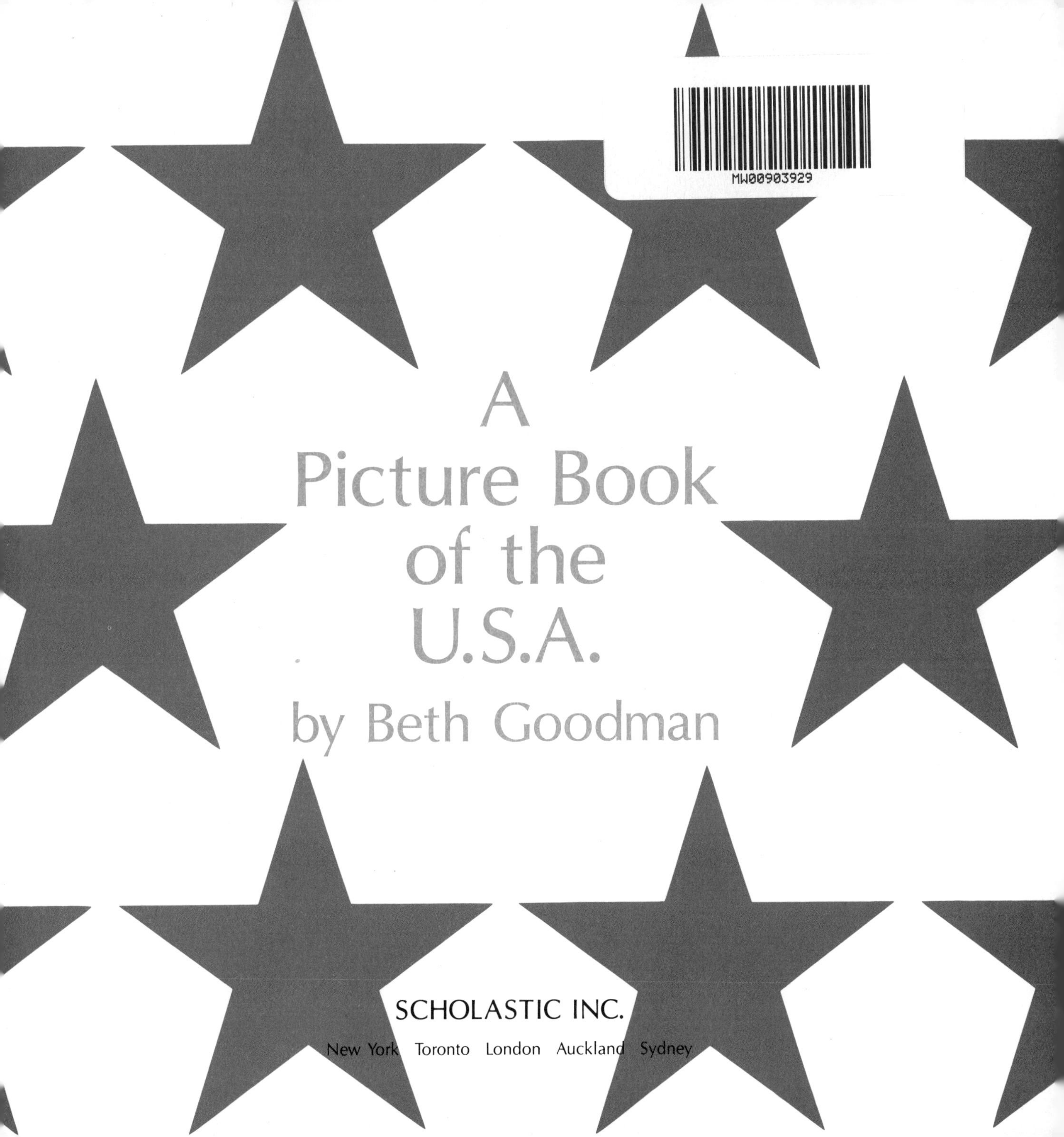

A Picture Book of the U.S.A.

by Beth Goodman

SCHOLASTIC INC.
New York Toronto London Auckland Sydney

ISBN 0-590-43909-X

12 11 10 9 8 3 4 5/9

Printed in the U.S.A. 24

First Scholastic printing, January 1991

Photos: *Desert Island, Maine:* © Superstock/Four by Five; *Vermont:* © Vermont Travel Division; *Martha's Vineyard:* © Leo de Wys/Stan Ries; *5th Avenue, New York:* © Superstock/Four by Five; *New Jersey:* © Leo de Wys; *Pittsburgh:* © Superstock/Four by Five; *Thoroughbred Yearlings:* © Leo de Wys/George Munday; *Miami Beach:* © MIWAKO IKEDA/Int'l. Stock Photo; *The White House:* © Leo de Wys/Fridmar Damm; *Wheat Field:* © Leo de Wys/Everett Johnson; *Mount Rushmore:* © Leo de Wys/Henryk Kaiser; *Rocky Mountain National Park:* © Leo de Wys/William P. Kraus; *Aspen, Colorado:* © Leo de Wys/Robert G. Hadden; *Wyoming:* © Leo de Wys/Steve Vidler; *Texas Pumpjacks:* © Leo de Wys/Bob Thomason; *The Grand Canyon:* © Leo de Wys/Steve Vidler; *San Francisco:* © Leo de Wys/James Hackett; *Mount Rainier:* © Superstock/Four by Five; *Alaska Glacier:* © Superstock/Four by Five; *Aloha Luau:* © Superstock/Four by Five

The United States is made up of 50 states and the District of Columbia, our nation's capital. Some states are famous for their bustling cities. Other states are known for their tree-covered mountains. Still other states are filled with miles and miles of rich farmland. The pictures in this book will give you a close-up look at the many different areas that make up the United States of America!

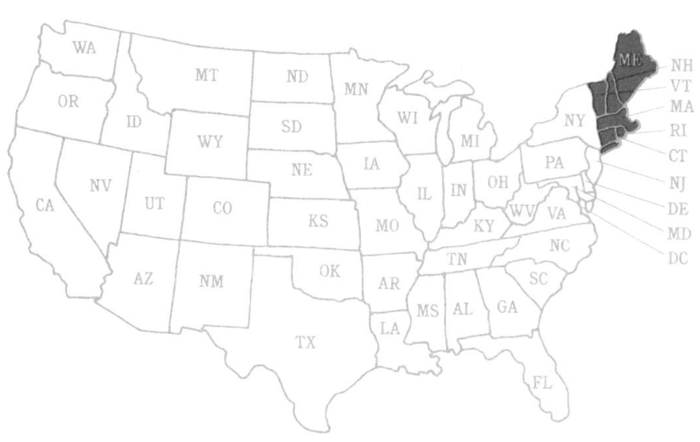

THE NEW ENGLAND STATES

The New England states are: Connecticut, Maine, Massachusetts, New Hampshire, Rhode Island, and Vermont.

The states that make up New England are known for their small, quaint, ocean-side villages and pretty mountain scenery. Many of the people who came to North America from England hundreds of years ago settled here. That is why the area is named New England.

Maine fishermen catch lobsters in wooden traps.

The maple syrup in Vermont is known to be the best in the country! These men are gathering sap from maple trees. The sap will be made into syrup.

These "gingerbread" houses are on Martha's Vineyard. Martha's Vineyard is a tiny island that is part of Massachusetts. Very few people live on Martha's Vineyard in the winter. Most of the homes on the island are summer homes.

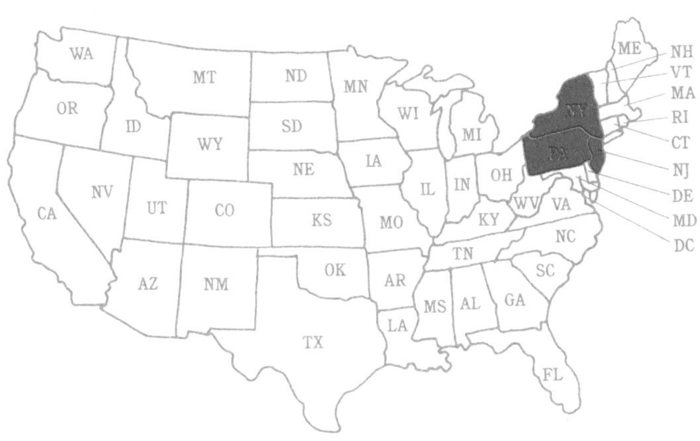

THE MIDDLE ATLANTIC STATES

The Middle Atlantic states are: New Jersey, New York, and Pennsylvania.

The Middle Atlantic States are more crowded with people than the states in any other part of the country. Over the years people have come from all over the world to live in New Jersey, New York, and Pennsylvania.

The many streets of New York City are packed with people rushing from one place to another.

New Jersey is called the "Garden State." It has acres of rich farmland where fruits and vegetables are grown.

A lot of people who live in Pittsburgh, Pennsylvania, work in steel mills. Workers use this machine to melt down steel.

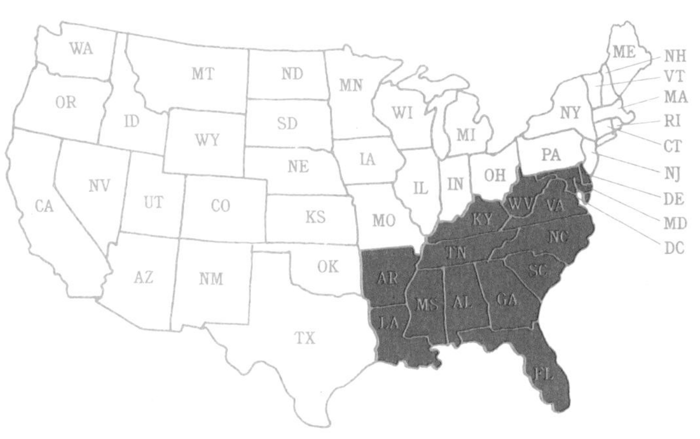

THE SOUTHERN STATES

The Southern states are: Alabama, Arkansas, Delaware, Florida, Georgia, Kentucky, Louisiana, Maryland, Mississippi, North Carolina, South Carolina, Tennessee, Virginia, and West Virginia.

In the Southern states are areas of flat land. There are also hills and mountains. Miles of beautiful beaches lie along the Atlantic Ocean and the Gulf of Mexico. The Southern states are known for their warm climates. In the wintertime, Southern beaches are popular vacation spots.

Raising horses is important in Kentucky. A big horse race called the Kentucky Derby is held in Louisville, Kentucky, every year in May.

Huge hotels line the crowded beaches in Miami Beach, Florida.

The District of Columbia is a city set aside from all of the states. It is our nation's capital.

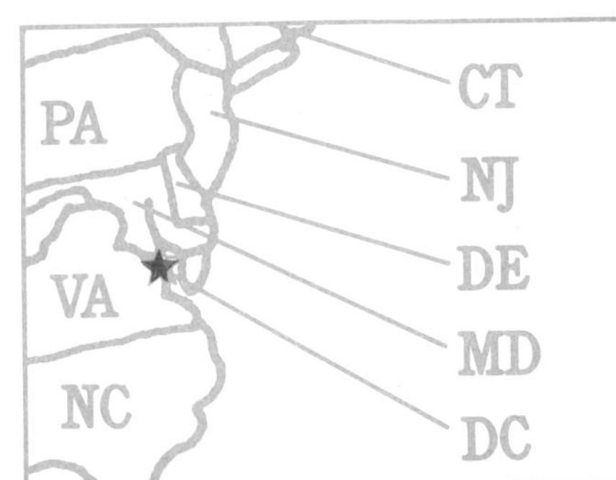

This is a picture of the White House. Every president of the United States has lived here since the nation's second president, John Adams.

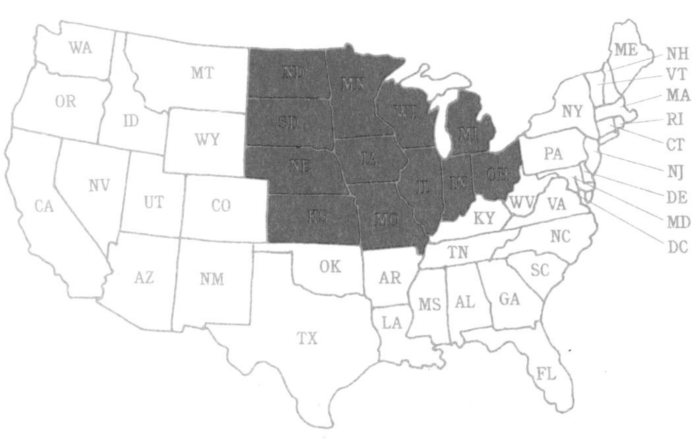

THE MIDWESTERN STATES

The Midwestern states are: Illinois, Indiana, Iowa, Kansas, Michigan, Minnesota, Missouri, Nebraska, North Dakota, Ohio, South Dakota, and Wisconsin.

There are huge areas of very flat land in the Midwest. This flat land covers most of the center of the country. Corn, wheat, and other crops grow on farms in these states. There are many dairy and animal farms in the Midwest. There are also bustling cities such as Chicago, Illinois.

Wheat fields in Illinois go on for as far as the eye can see! The wheat in this field will soon be ready to be harvested.

The Mount Rushmore National Memorial was carved out of a stony mountainside in South Dakota. The faces are of past United States presidents George Washington, Thomas Jefferson, Theodore Roosevelt, and Abraham Lincoln. Each of the faces are 60 feet long!

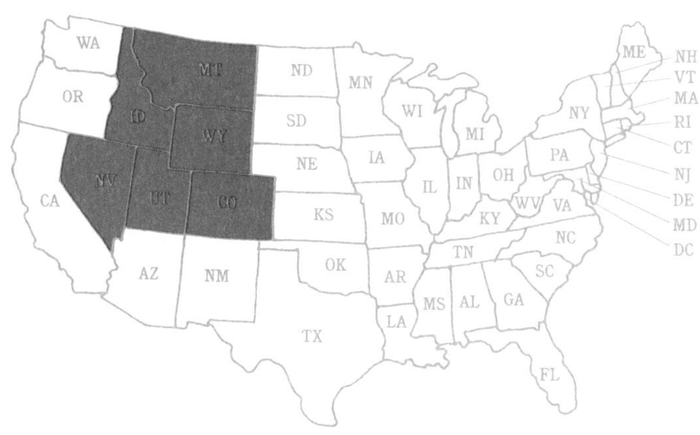

THE ROCKY MOUNTAIN STATES

The Rocky Mountain states are: Colorado, Idaho, Montana, Nevada, Utah, and Wyoming.

The Rocky Mountains cut through all of the states in this area of the country. But along with the rugged, mountainous areas, there are also deserts and flat plains to be found in the Rocky Mountain states. A large part of the Rocky Mountains area is a wilderness where only a small number of people live.

The Rocky Mountain range is more than 3,000 miles long. In some areas it is 350 miles wide! Many wild animals, such as moose, mountain lions, bears, and goats, live in these mountains.

People love to ski on the steep and beautiful mountains in Aspen, Colorado.

Yellowstone National Park in Wyoming is the country's oldest national park. It has many natural hot springs and geysers. Wild animals such as this buffalo roam freely in parts of the park!

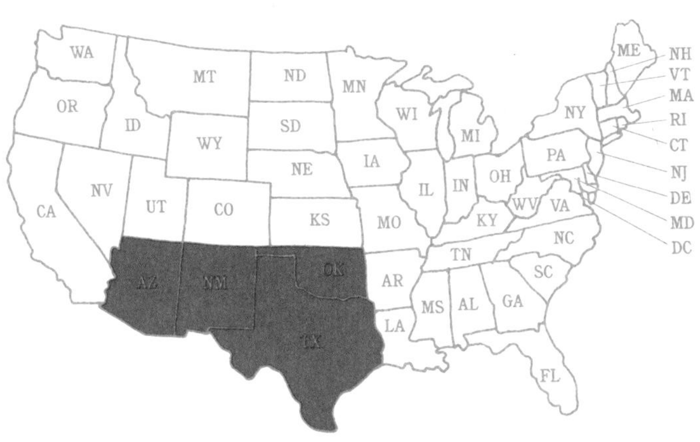

THE SOUTHWESTERN STATES

The Southwestern states are: Arizona, New Mexico, Oklahoma, and Texas.

Sometimes the Southwestern states are called the "wide open spaces." There are huge ranches where cattle roam, and large fields where cotton grows. The weather is usually sunny and dry.

There are many oil fields in the Southwest. Oil has brought the Southwestern states most of their money.

These big pumpjacks help pump the oil out of the ground.

The Grand Canyon in Arizona is the largest canyon in the world. It is 227 miles long! Some people ride mules down into the canyon. Others may take a raft ride on the Colorado River, which flows into the canyon.

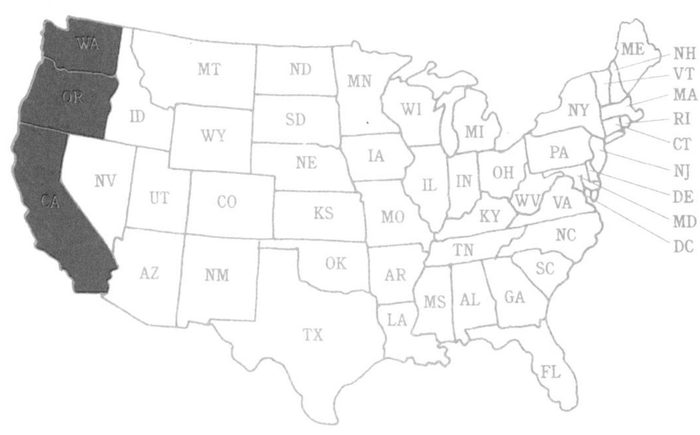

THE PACIFIC COAST STATES

The Pacific Coast states are: California, Oregon, and Washington.

California, Oregon, and Washington all border the Pacific Ocean. These states are known for their miles and miles of beautiful beaches, thick forests, and mountains. The weather in this region is usually mild, so outdoor sports such as surfing and hiking are very popular.

Lots of vegetables, nuts, and fruits, especially grapes, are grown in this area.

Trolley cars carry people up and down the hilly streets of San Francisco, California.

Mount Rainier is in Washington. It stands 14,410 feet high!

ALASKA

Alaska is the largest of all the 50 states. It borders Canada and lies in the Pacific and Arctic oceans. Alaska is rich in fish, minerals, and timber.

Many glaciers can be found in Alaska. They form in valleys and canyons and can be as small as one mile, or as wide as 30 miles!

HAWAII

Hawaii is made up of 20 islands. It lies in the Pacific Ocean, about 2,400 miles off the coast of San Francisco. The weather in Hawaii is tropical, and many beautiful plants and flowers grow there. Pineapples, coffee beans, and sugar are some of the state's main crops.

These women are hula dancers. They are performing at a Hawaiian luau. A luau is a ceremony that includes lots of music, dancing, and eating.